The Nature in Close-up Series

Taylor, Keith
  Foxes.—(Nature in close-up; 17)
  1. Foxes—Juvenile literature
  I. Title   II. Series
  599.74'442   QL737.C22
  ISBN 0-7136-2294-6

Published by A & C Black (Publishers) Limited
35 Bedford Row, London WC1R 4JH

First published 1983

Filmset by August Filmsetting, Warrington, Cheshire
Printed in Hong Kong by Dai Nippon Printing Co. Ltd

Nature in Close-up

FOXES

Keith Taylor
Photographs by David Grewcock

Adam & Charles Black · London

Contents

Introduction

Look at this picture of a red fox. What does it remind you of? Foxes and wolves are both related to dogs.

Foxes, dogs and wolves are all *carnivores*. Carnivore means 'meat-eater'. Foxes usually eat meat, but they will eat berries, fruit, eggs and even grass if they can't find any meat.

There are lots of different kinds of fox. The red fox is the most common. It can be found all over Europe, North Africa, North America and most of Asia.

Red foxes live in all sorts of places; in woodland, moorland, or on farms. Some foxes even live in towns. This book will tell you where you might find red foxes, how they live and breed and how they manage to survive.

Tracks and signs

The best way to find out about foxes is to watch them. Red foxes are very shy. They come out at night and hide during the day, so they're hard to find. But you might see the tracks and signs they leave behind.

Here are some clues which tell you that a fox might be nearby.

You may be able to spot a fox's paw prints in muddy ground. These are an oval shape, about 5 cm long and 4 cm wide. A fox has four fleshy pads on its paws.

A fox's footprints are in a single line. This is because of the way the fox walks. It puts one front paw down first. Then it puts one back paw into the footprint left by the front paw.

▲ Fox's scat (top), hedgehog dropping (left) and owl pellet (bottom)

Another way of finding foxes is to look for their droppings, called *scats*. Compare the fox scat in this picture with the owl pellet and the hedgehog dropping. A fox scat has a point at each end. The bits of bone in this scat tell us that the fox has been eating birds, mice and voles. What has the owl been eating?

If you are lucky, you may find a fox's *earth*. This is the underground tunnel where the female fox (vixen) hides during the daytime. The vixen usually digs her earth in October. She often uses tunnels left by badgers or rabbits. Foxes are very untidy, so you might see scats and left-over bits of food outside the earth.

Foxes in close-up

The fox is about the same size as a spaniel dog, but the fox's long bushy tail makes it look much bigger. The male fox (dog fox) is usually bigger than the vixen and has a broader face.

The tail is often called a 'brush'. A fox uses its tail rather like a scarf. When a fox goes to sleep, it wraps its tail round its body and face to keep warm. Many foxes have a white tip to their tail.

The fur. A fox has two different kinds of fur. The underfur keeps the fox warm. It's a bluish-grey colour and is very fluffy. In autumn, the underfur grows thicker to protect the fox from the cold.

The outer fur is made of lots of long hairs, called guard hairs. These hairs keep the underfur dry. They also give the fox its red-brown colour. Foxes spend a lot of time cleaning their fur with their tongue and paws.

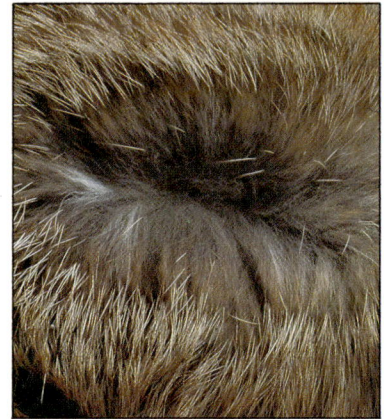

▲ Underfur

▲ Outer fur

The teeth. You can tell that foxes are carnivores by looking at their teeth. A fox has forty two teeth altogether. Four of these are very long and pointed. They are called *canines* and are used for biting and tearing. The fox has six smaller teeth at the front of its top and bottom jaw. These are used for cutting bits of food into small pieces. The rest of the teeth are used for grinding food until it is small enough to swallow.

Nose, eyes, ears and whiskers

Foxes have to hunt for food. They need sharp senses to find their prey. Usually, foxes hunt at night. Which senses do you think they use the most?

Look at this picture of a fox hunting. Its ears are pricked forward. It is listening for small animals to hunt. Foxes have very sharp ears. They can hear a mouse or a bird moving from a long way away. They point their ears backwards or forwards to find out where a noise is coming from.

Foxes have a very keen sense of smell, too. They sniff along the ground and follow the scent which other animals leave behind. They also sniff the air to find out which animals are nearby.

A healthy fox always has a wet nose. Try licking your finger and holding it up in the air. You will be able to feel which way the wind is blowing. A fox uses its wet nose in the same way, so it knows where a smell is coming from.

A fox's whiskers give it an important extra sense. When a fox wants to get through a small gap, it puts its nose in first. If its whiskers touch the sides of the hole, the fox knows that its body won't fit through.

Foxes don't have very good eyesight. They can only see moving objects, or things which are nearby. But they can see almost as well in the dark as they do in the daytime. Can you see the fox's eyes glowing in the dark? At night, a fox's pupils are big and round. This helps the fox to see better. During the day, the pupils are narrow slits so they don't let in too much light.

Finding food

Foxes are supposed to be very cunning hunters. There are lots of stories about the tricks they play on other animals. Some people say that foxes pretend to be dead, then jump up and catch any animals which come too close. But no-one knows if these stories are true or not.

Rabbits used to be the fox's most important food. But rabbits aren't as common as they used to be. Many of them have died of a disease called *myxomatosis*. Foxes have learned to hunt other animals, such as mice, birds, voles or frogs. They catch these animals by pouncing on them with their front paws. The fox uses its paws to hold down its prey. Then it kills the animal by biting it on the back of the head.

If they can't find any meat, foxes will eat insects, fruit, berries or even grass. Logs and old tree stumps are a good place to find beetles and grubs. The fox scrapes the cracks with its paws and snaps up any insects which crawl out.

Farmers don't like foxes because they steal chickens and ducks. Sometimes they steal eggs, too. The fox gently picks up an egg in its jaws and carries it to a safe place. It holds the egg in its paws, bites off the top and licks out the tasty insides.

▼ Carrying an egg to a safe place

▲ Burying food

Some farmers say that foxes will attack sheep. This is probably not true. Foxes only hunt small animals, unless they are very hungry. But they will eat any dead animals they find. Dead animals are called *carrion*.

When there is plenty of food, a fox will often bury some to eat later. It digs a hole in the ground and uses its nose to cover up the food with earth and leaves. The store is called a *cache*. Sometimes, the fox marks the spot with its smell so it can find the cache more easily.

In winter, food is often hard to find. Many of the insects have died. There are no berries and the ground is sometimes too hard for digging.

Small animals, like voles and mice, make tunnels under the snow. The fox waits until it hears an animal scuttling along one of these 'runs'. Then it starts to dig into the run. After a while, the fox stops, listens and starts to dig again. It may have to dig into lots of different runs before it finds enough to eat.

The mating season

In winter, the dog fox starts to look for a mate. When he finds a vixen, he barks loudly to her. Sometimes the vixen barks back. Sometimes, she makes a loud screaming noise. The two foxes call to each other with barks, screams, chattering and yelps.

The dog fox will fight any other male foxes who come too close to his mate. He puts a special scent on the patch of land around her earth. This tells other foxes that the land is his territory. It warns them to keep away.

▼ A fox calling to its mate

A dog fox marks a tree stump with its scent ▶

The dog fox's scent comes from a small gland under his tail, called the *anal gland*. The fox rubs his hindquarters against logs and rocks to mark them with his scent. A place which is marked like this is called a *scenting post*.

The vixen and her mate stay in their territory for most of the winter. The vixen lives in the earth and the dog fox makes *dens* to sleep in. These are small hollows scratched out of the ground in sheltered places. The dog fox makes several dens in his territory.

Fox cubs

About seven weeks after she has mated with the dog fox, the vixen gives birth to her cubs. She can have as many as eight cubs, but she usually has five or less.

The cubs are born blind. They don't open their eyes until they're about two weeks old. They stay in the earth and the vixen feeds them with her milk.

▼ A pregnant vixen hunting for food

When they're about four weeks old, the fox cubs leave the earth for the first time. They don't look much like foxes! Their eyes are blue and their coats are grey or brown. The cubs stay close to their mother and don't go far from the earth.

◀ A very young fox cub

After a few weeks, the cubs start to grow reddish fur. Their eyes slowly turn brown, too. The vixen brings them small animals to eat. At first, she breaks up the food with her jaws but the cubs are soon strong enough to do this for themselves.

◀ A six week old fox cub   17

Slowly the fox cubs learn to hunt for food. They learn the smells of the animals which the vixen brings back to the earth. Sometimes, the cubs keep a pheasant wing or a rabbit skin to play with.

The cubs play with each other, too. They chase each other and have pretend fights. Running and fighting helps them to grow strong. One of their favourite games is 'pouncing'. One cub twitches its tail while another cub tries to pounce on the tail with its front paws. This is good practice for hunting. By the time the cubs are three months old, they have learned to pounce on mice and other small animals.

As the cubs learn to hunt, they go further and further away from the earth. They learn about all the different smells and noises around them. By autumn, they are ready to look after themselves. The young dog foxes leave home to make their own territories. The young vixens stay closer to home. They will make their earths near the mother fox. When winter comes, the young foxes will look for mates and have cubs of their own.

◄ Ten week old cubs playing outside their earth (main picture)
Eight week old cubs (left)
Nine week old cub (right)

The fox's enemies

Foxes don't have many enemies. They used to be hunted by wolves and bears. But now these animals only live in very wild places. The fox's main enemy is man.

Many people think foxes should be killed because they steal chickens and ducks from farms. If a fox gets into a hen house, it will often kill almost all the chickens living there. Foxes also kill other domestic animals, such as pheasant and partridge chicks, or sometimes even young lambs. This is why foxes are often shot or killed in traps.

Hunting on horseback

▲ Hounds following a fox's scent

▲ A fox caught in a snare

Hunting with hounds is another way of controlling the number of foxes which live in the countryside. The hounds follow the scent of the fox and the hunters follow the hounds on horseback. Poison is also used to kill foxes. Sometimes, people dig up the foxes' earths and kill the cubs.

Foxes can be a nuisance and many people think we should make sure that there aren't too many of them. But the way that this is done is often very cruel.

21

Foxes in towns and suburbs

Many wild animals are hard to find now. People aren't allowed to kill them. Foxes are still common, even though they're hunted and killed. They have survived because they are adaptable. They can learn to live in different ways. For example, if a fox can't find one kind of food it will learn to find something else to eat.

Foxes can live in all sorts of different places. They even live in towns and suburbs. Many of the fields and woods where foxes used to live have gone. Houses and roads have been built on them. But the foxes haven't moved away. They've learned to live near people and buildings.

These foxes make their homes in park shrubberies, churchyards and wasteland. Sometimes they choose railway embankments or the bottom of a quiet garden.

Foxes in towns and suburbs are safe from hunters. There is plenty of food for them, too. Have you ever had your dustbins raided? It might have been a fox looking for scraps of food. Town foxes often tip over dustbins or steal food from rubbish tips. They also catch mice, rats and garden birds.

In quiet suburbs, foxes will sometimes come out during the day. This fox is sunbathing. Foxes and cubs have been seen drinking from bird baths or ponds in people's gardens. At night, you might even see them in the centre of towns, so watch out for them!

Index